# Mighty Machines

WITHDRAWN # Destroyers

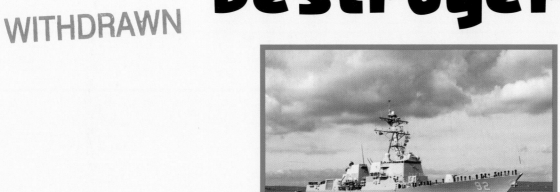

by Matt Doeden

Consulting Editor: Gail Saunders-Smith, PhD

Capstone press

Mankato, Minnesota

Pebble Plus is published by Capstone Press,
151 Good Counsel Drive, P.O. Box 669, Mankato, Minnesota 56002.
www.capstonepress.com

1 2 3 4 5 6 12 11 10 09 08 07

*Library of Congress Cataloging-in-Publication Data*
Doeden, Matt.
    Destroyers / by Matt Doeden.
    p. cm.— (Pebble Plus. Mighty machines.)
    Includes bibliographical references and index.
    ISBN-13: 978-1-4296-0029-3 (hardcover)
    ISBN-10: 1-4296-0029-2 (hardcover)
    1. Destroyers (Warships)—Juvenile literature. I. Title. II. Series.
V825.D63 2008
623.825'4—dc22                                                                    2006101114

Summary: Simple text and photographs describe destroyers, their parts, and what they do.

**Editorial Credits**
Mari Schuh and Christopher L. Harbo, editors; Patrick D. Dentinger, book designer; Jo Miller, photo researcher

**Photo Credits**
DVIC/Paul Farley, 9; PH2 Timothy Smith, 17; PH3 Aramis X. Ramirez, cover; PH3 Yesenia Rosas, 15;
    PHAN Stephen W. Rowe, 7
U.S. Navy Photo by JO3 Ryan C. McGinley, 21; MC2 John L. Beeman, 19; PH1 Michael W. Pendergrass, 13;
    PH1 Ted Banks, 11; PH3 Douglas G. Morrison, 1; PH3 John Sullivan, 5

**Capstone Press thanks Dr. Sarandis Papadopoulos, Naval Historian, for his assistance with this book.**

## Note to Parents and Teachers

The Mighty Machines set supports national social studies standards related to science, technology, and society. This book describes and illustrates destroyers. The images support early readers in understanding the text. The repetition of words and phrases helps early readers learn new words. This book also introduces early readers to subject-specific vocabulary words, which are defined in the Glossary section. Early readers may need assistance to read some words and to use the Table of Contents, Glossary, Read More, Internet Sites, and Index sections of the book.

# Table of Contents

# What Are Destroyers?

Destroyers are

fast warships.

Destroyers protect

larger Navy ships

from enemies.

# Destroyer Parts

The main body of a destroyer is called the hull.
Steel plates form the hull.

hull

The mast holds most
of the ship's instruments.

mast

Destroyers carry
cannons, missiles,
and torpedoes.

cannon

Most destroyers

have a helicopter pad.

Helicopters take off

and land on the pad.

# Destroyer Crews

Crews work on destroyers.

Officers lead the crews.

Crew members control

the destroyer's instruments.

Gunners shoot at

enemy ships and aircraft.

# Mighty Machines

Destroyers protect
the Navy's ships.
Destroyers are
mighty machines.

# Glossary

cannon—a large gun that shoots bullets a long distance

gunner—a crew member who shoots a vehicle's guns or missiles

hull—the main body of a ship; destroyers have steel hulls.

instrument—a tool that gets information; destroyers have instruments called radar and sonar to detect enemies above and below the water.

mast—the part of a destroyer that rises high above the hull; the mast contains most of the ship's instruments.

missile—an explosive that flies through the air

navy—the military sea force of a country, including ships, aircraft, weapons, land bases, and people

officer—a person who gives orders to other people in the armed forces

torpedo—an explosive that travels underwater

# Read More

**Armentrout, David, and Patricia Armentrout.** *Ships.* Transportation. Vero Beach, Fla.: Rourke, 2004.

**Doeden, Matt.** *The U.S. Navy.* The U.S. Armed Forces. Mankato, Minn.: Capstone Press, 2005.

**Rustad, Martha E. H.** *U.S. Navy Destroyers.* Military Vehicles. Mankato, Minn.: Capstone Press, 2007.

# Internet Sites

FactHound offers a safe, fun way to find Internet sites related to this book. All of the sites on FactHound have been researched by our staff.

Here's how:

1. Visit *www.facthound.com*

2. Choose your grade level.

3. Type in this book ID **1429600292** for age-appropriate sites. You may also browse subjects by clicking on letters, or by clicking on pictures and words.

4. Click on the **Fetch It** button.

**FactHound will fetch the best sites for you!**

# Index

Word Count: 84
Grade: 1
Early-Intervention Level: 16